100 WORDS OF affirmation YOUR SON

NEEDS TO HEAR

Also by Matt and Lisa Jacobson

100 WORDS OF affirmation YOUR SON NEEDS TO HEAR

Matt Jacobson
and
Lisa Jacobson

Revell

a division of Baker Publishing Group
Grand Rapids, Michigan

© 2021 by Faithful Families Ministries, LLC

Published by Revell
a division of Baker Publishing Group
PO Box 6287, Grand Rapids, MI 49516-6287
www.revellbooks.com

Printed in the United States of America

Library of Congress Cataloging-in-Publication Data
Names: Jacobson, Matt, author. | Jacobson, Lisa, author.
Title: 100 words of affirmation your son needs to hear / Matt Jacobson and Lisa Jacobson.
Description: Grand Rapids, Michigan : Revell, a division of Baker Publishing Group,
    [2021]
Identifiers: LCCN 2020046205 | ISBN 9780800739454 (paperback) | ISBN 9780800740719
    (casebound)
Subjects: LCSH: Parent and child—Religious aspects—Christianity. | Sons. | Boys—
    Religious life. | Encouragement—Religious aspects—Christianity. | Positive
    psychology.
Classification: LCC BV4529 .J3285 2021 | DDC 248.8/45—dc23
LC record available at https://lccn.loc.gov/2020046205

21 22 23 24 25 26 27   7 6 5 4 3 2 1

green
press
INITIATIVE

Introduction

You love your son, right? But do you *like* your son? And more important, does he *know* you like him? What have you done to communicate that to your son?

You might have deep feelings for him, but that's not enough. He doesn't necessarily know what you know or how keenly you feel. When was the last time you spoke words of affirmation directly to him? Have you regularly found the goodness in the moments of your son's life and commented, even raved, about them?

He needs to hear from you, and *100 Words of Affirmation Your Son Needs to Hear* is a resource to spark your thinking and help you look for those times when you can speak positive words of encouragement, success, and destiny into his heart.

This book will encourage you to find everyday wins in your son's life and celebrate those wins in real time. The world will tear him down, but you have the gift to lift him up. Use your powerful voice as a parent to speak words of affirmation into his heart and begin building your relationship on a positive, unshakable foundation.

1

I have great *confidence* in your future.

Our son was busy with his usual morning chore of collecting eggs from the nests in the chicken coop, carrying a few dozen into the house, and then washing them in the laundry room sink. Maybe it felt special when he first took over "Farm Boy Fresh Eggs," but such jobs quickly lose their glamour and become mundane to a young kid like him, whose eyes are on the horizon, ready to take on the world.

He grew up with a father who encouraged diligence and endurance, but on that morning, I watched from a short distance away with a mother's eye, perceiving things he was blind to in that moment. I spotted big stuff in his little faithfulness. And I told him so.

"Son, God has great things planned for your future."

He looked up at me, eyes wide with surprise, nearly cracking an egg in the process. He was amazed to have been noticed and was startled by my morning prophecy.

But, of course, I meant it. From where he stood, he was simply washing dried chicken poop from eggshells. But from where I stood, he was a young man going places, one speckled brown egg at a time.

Many days in a son's life involve simply putting one foot in front of the other—being diligent and faithful to finish the job at hand. And it's times like these when you, as his parent, have the opportunity to instill a vision for his future. You will often see more than your son has the maturity or capacity to comprehend. Life may seem mundane or even bleak at times, but your confidence in his future is strong, isn't it? Show him how his diligence and faithfulness are connected to the future God already has planned for him.

You're the kind of *friend* I wanted when I was your age.

There may come a time in your son's life when finding genuine friends proves difficult. People are often fickle and self-interested. True friends are hard to come by. Faithfulness, loyalty, and selflessness are too often in short supply.

If your son finds himself going through a lonely season, the messages from the enemy can be very discouraging: *You're not worth it. You're not cool enough. Nobody wants to be your friend.* But you're nearby, and when the world tells him he has little value, you can tell him the truth—he's an awesome friend, and one you would have loved to have had when you were his age. Tell him you're not just his dad or mom; you're his friend and confidant.

Also, be sure to point him to Jesus, who knew what it meant to be betrayed by His closest companions until He was utterly alone. Jesus understands. He was attacked by friends who pretended they didn't know Him in order to save themselves. But He will never abandon us. He's forever faithful, and that's important to know when you have to spend a night or two—or a season—in life's lonely valley.

God *blessed* me by bringing you into the world.

Some people might have considered me too old to be having a baby. I was forty, after all, when I had our youngest. And I wouldn't be sharing honestly if I didn't say that I'd occasionally had the thought during that pregnancy, *What am I doing having a baby at this age?*

But then he was born. Our handsome blue-eyed boy with the sweetest temperament you can imagine. How could I have ever doubted?

So I tell him. I want him to know what a gift he is and how his hugs and silly antics bring me such cheer. If I don't tell him, how will he know?

If you think back to when you were young, you'll probably remember how insignificant kids can feel. Sometimes they believe they don't really matter all that much. But the truth is, they mean the world!

Tell your child how much he means to you and how thankful you are that God brought him into your life.

You offer such comfort with your *gentle strength.*

Sunday was an unusually hard day. Right in the middle of prayer time at church, our daughter with special needs suffered a grand mal seizure, and suddenly everything came to a standstill. Everyone watched helplessly while she cried out loudly in pain and her body trembled with the violence of an earthquake.

Matt is typically at her side in an instant, but he was traveling that weekend. Because my eyes had been closed in prayer, it took me a few moments to get my bearings before jumping up and rushing to reach her wheelchair at the end of our row. But I was second to arrive, as her younger brother was already by her side, wrapping her tightly in strong, loving arms to calm her convulsions. I joined him, and the two of us held on to her for a long minute and a half until the tremors subsided.

When the seizure was over at last, he disappeared. Was he alright? I was worried, but then he returned with a tissue to wipe the tears from her eyes and the drool from her face. At that point I could no longer keep it together, so he made another trip to the bathroom—this time to get more tissues for me.

He's only a young teen, but he somehow knew just what to do right then. His gentle strength in that sad and difficult situation brought both his sister and me such comfort.

Perhaps your son won't have to step into such a challenging moment, or maybe he deals with even greater trauma. But there will be times in your son's life when he rises to offer himself in difficult moments. It's unlikely he will understand how much comfort he brings you and the rest of his family with his thoughtfulness, gentle strength, or kindness, which is why he needs to hear from you what an awesome blessing he really is!

You faced a big challenge, yet you *refused* to give up.

His freshman year of high school, our son decided to join the local Christian school's basketball team. He went to every practice, every drill, and every game. And if you know anything about playing for a small school, you know this means driving for hours and hours to remote, faraway tournaments. It's a monumental time commitment.

Despite all of that time and effort, he spent virtually the entire season sitting on the bench, playing only a few minutes—and only when it didn't matter.

As his dad, I held my peace but found myself getting a little frustrated that the coaches didn't play him more (like every dad on the planet!). And Lisa got a little emotional. We believe in perseverance and encouraged him to endure when other boys in the same situation were quitting, but we both began to wonder how this continuing negative experience would affect him.

Then one day at the end of the season, on the way home from another game that he spent on the bench, he said to me, "Dad, I don't want to keep sitting on the bench. I want to play."

"Well, son, you don't have to. You have what it takes to succeed. The question is, are you willing to do the work and discipline yourself enough to achieve your goal? The opportunity is there and you can have it, but are you willing to do what it takes?"

"Yes, I am!" he answered with resolution.

"Okay, then here's what you have to do. We'll get you with a coach who will truly teach you, and then the rest is up to you. Incidentally, what is your specific goal?"

"I want to start every game."

So he practiced and practiced. When I was heading to bed at

11:00 p.m., I'd walk past him sitting on the stairs, lacing up his shoes. Another night the rain beat down, but it couldn't drown out the *thump, thump* of his dribbling the basketball through hazard cones as he drove to the basket.

Sheer determination.

Did his perseverance pay off? Yes, it did. The next season he became a top-three starter!

Perhaps your son is too young to be on a sports team, or maybe his interests lie elsewhere. The "what" isn't important. Encourage him to be his best, and help him see a pathway to pursue his goals. And don't be hesitant to start young. Did he put away all his blocks? That's fantastic! Tell him how much you appreciate his tenacity, and then whisper how such commitment leads to bigger things later in life.

I love hearing your *ideas* and *dreams* for the future.

Life has a way of beating dreams out of young men. That's why your son needs to know you're genuinely interested in his ideas, aspirations, and thoughts about impossible deeds. When I was young, I thought I would be a policeman, a cowboy, a boxer, then . . . you name it and I thought about being it. Kids have all kinds of wonderful, wild, crazy thoughts. Then they become teenagers and still have them. Don't be the parent with all the reasons "why not." Be the parent who invites conversation about the possibilities.

I still remember talking with my mother when I was eighteen about my "plans"—my big plans to become a professional boxer. Inside, she was probably thinking, *I don't want my son to have his brains bashed in!* But she just sat there smiling and listening with enrapt interest as I told her all about my intentions. (It's Sugar Ray Leonard's fault.) The only problem was . . . well, just about everything. But that didn't make her stomp on my thoughts. If I was excited about it, she was excited to hear about it. And to this day, I have an untarnished record as a boxer! Zero wins, zero losses. Ha ha. Thanks, Mom!

No, I didn't get into the ring, ever, and that dream floated into thin air along with so many others. Your son was also created with a dream. Perhaps it is to become a hero, fight a battle, climb a mountain, be a world-class musician, win first prize at 4-H, or cross the sea into uncharted waters. Whatever his dream is, let him know that you love hearing about it and believe he can achieve it.

Son, that was a *kind* thing to do.

I'm sure I'm not the only mom who, at times, has trouble finding her tweenage sons! Today was one of those days. I walked through the house searching for our son but didn't see him in his usual spots. He was supposed to be finishing up his schoolwork, but I could hear him laughing and finally found him in the kitchen. And it's not as though he was busy eating a midmorning snack either. Instead, he was sitting at the kitchen table playing a rousing game of Uno with his sister.

It sounds irresponsible, I know, except he was playing with his sister with special needs who's in a wheelchair. She doesn't necessarily have many opportunities for fun, and his heart went out to her, so he thought it might be a nice break to suggest they play a card game together.

I quietly watched the two from across the room. She'd laugh as she laid down some penalty card for him, and then he'd draw a fistful of cards, moaning loudly to make her laugh even harder. It was a regular circus. He was (purposefully) losing badly—and she couldn't have been more tickled about it.

I thought about what his report card might look like at the end of the year. Would he get good grades? Probably, since he was doing reasonably well in his academics. But I also wondered why we're so ready to recognize grades and wins but easily overlook the important things like love and kindness.

I suggest that if you catch your son doing something sacrificial or kind, quickly acknowledge it. In a world that strongly commends strength and achievement, don't lose sight of the immense value of loving another person.

I *believe* the hand of God is on your life.

Life will offer your son many opportunities to doubt that God is involved in his world, is watching over him, or even cares. When he is young, his doubts will be few, but life has a way of increasing them as he gets older.

You don't have to wait for a magic moment, a special occasion, or some great tragedy or challenge to speak words of destiny and hope into your son's heart. The ordinary, everyday moments are the best times to remind him of what he'll need to hang on to at some point: God is present, God has a plan, and God has a purpose in everything.

It's an important truth to have settled in his mind before life throws him a curveball. And it is a truth to know—something the Bible is crystal clear about. God is at work in every aspect of our lives, shaping us (if we let Him), refining us, and molding us into the people He wants us to be.

If you regularly speak this kind of vision into your son's heart, he will be better equipped to handle the highs and lows he will be sure to encounter.

You have a *terrific* sense of humor.

It's settled! Our youngest son's mission in life is to make us laugh. And if one of his antics succeeds, it's guaranteed that we'll get whatever it was he did on repeat for several weeks (if not months) to come!

For instance, we made the terrible mistake of giggling at his rendition of "My Baby Elf"—one of those Silly Songs with Larry. Admittedly, it's an amusing song, but honestly, by the fifth time he gets to the "my elfity, babity, babity, babity, babity, babity elf" part (in his best thirteen-year-old Elvis imperson-ation), our sanity comes into question. Yet, even so, we can hardly help laughing.

But do you want to know what we've learned about these silly moments? They aren't nearly so much about amusement; they're about love. Our laughing at his jokes and juvenile comedy routine is just another way of saying "I think you're wonderful."

Delight in your son's jokes and wit. Tell him you think he's funny, clever, hilarious . . . or whatever fits. It's a small, easy way to build his confidence and express appreciation for his unique sense of humor. It also builds something else deeply important as he progresses into young adulthood: friendship.

What you decide to do today is building the *future* you will enjoy.

Much of life is about putting one foot in front of the other—being faithful in the little things. Whether it's taking out the trash for the thousandth time or completing some other mundane chore, wise parents help their sons see the connection between faithfulness today and a bright future tomorrow, between the unremarkable and the destiny God has planned for them.

Speak purpose, meaning, and a hopeful future into your son's day. It's difficult for a child to understand the value of doing simple, everyday tasks with excellence; that's where vision comes in. Show him the connection today has to the journey he's on and the exciting destination it may lead to.

You might start by saying, "Hey, son, that's a boring job, isn't it?" There's nothing wrong with honesty! But then you can give him a picture of what it means to provide an example for others—his brothers and sisters, and then, how about those future employees he might have one day?

Every effective leader leads by example.

Explain to your son that even—*especially*—when no one is looking (except God), the way he disciplines himself is how he will lead others. And because everything we do is open to God's appraisal, although we might not plan to lead others in a business endeavor someday, we should remember that we are instructed to work "as to the Lord," as it says in Colossians 3:23–24: "And whatsoever ye do, do it heartily, as to the Lord, and not unto men; Knowing that of the Lord ye shall receive the reward of the inheritance: for ye serve the Lord Christ" (KJV).

I *admire* the kind of man you're becoming.

Our fifteen-year-old was in the middle of a project when the phone rang. It was Matt's dad, who was in hospice care but living next door to us on our property. Matt was his primary caregiver but could step away to take care of other business for short periods of time. And sometimes all the different needs clashed with one another. That phone call was Dad telling us he needed help with another severe nosebleed (they often lasted four hours or more), but Matt couldn't get there for at least a half hour. I stood up to run next door and see what I could do when our son stopped me. "I can take care of this, Mom," he said firmly. "Let me go over."

I hesitated, knowing he was in the middle of schoolwork, and, besides, it would likely be a messy job. But he insisted.

Later his grandpa told us what a champion his grandson had been, and my heart soared. The first chance I got, I passed on to our son what a blessing he'd been to his grandfather and added what a blessing he'd been to me as well.

"Son, I admire the kind of man you are becoming."

This is just an example of our son in a specific situation. It will be different with yours, but surely you've noticed something about him you can call attention to: his kindness, thoughtfulness, or dependability?

Focus on the character quality he's growing in or has demonstrated, and then make the most of it. Point it out to him. Applaud him for it. Admire the man he's becoming.

You have an *important* place in this family.

Ask any expert on gangs and youth about how and why kids join, and with little variation, you'll get the same answer: gangs fulfill the need for family and a sense of belonging in the lives of young boys.

Boys need a tribe. Your son may not be heading out to join a gang, but does he know, down to the innermost place in his heart, that he belongs and has an essential place in your family? It's not a question of how you feel but of how your son sees himself.

There are two powerful ways to reinforce the importance of your son's place, his belonging in your family. What is the consistent message he receives from you? What is the percentage of positive affirmation he receives from you on a daily basis compared to negative or neutral comments? If the messaging in your home were analyzed, what would the report say?

Discipline yourself to regularly tell your son, "You are so important to us, and you have a powerful place in our family." Words are good, vital, and important, but there is another strong element to a son believing in the value of his place in his family: contribution.

I grew up in Canada, splitting wood as a young boy in the interior of British Columbia to stave off the long, bitterly cold winter. It wasn't a job to me. I love splitting wood. It's still in my bones to this day, but ever since our oldest was about nine, even though we have a fireplace in our home we use nearly every winter day, I haven't split a single round of firewood (unless for pleasure!) or stacked it or carried it into the house or started the fire in the morning, unless I just had the urge to do so. My boys—my young men—have handled it. It's real work, and they take it seriously. And I take them seriously, telling them what a valuable contribution they are making to the family by building a blazing fire to keep their mom warm. They know they are contributing greatly to how the home is run.

Along with your positive words, is there something you could give your son to do? Find something that would allow you to point out that he is making a genuine contribution and you sincerely appreciate his efforts.

Your thankful spirit is a true *encouragement* to me.

Maybe meatloaf isn't all that popular in your home, but it seems to be a favorite in ours—at least with our boys. (I should give you my recipe; the secret glaze is what makes it a real success!)

So when our seventeen-year-old son finished his meatloaf dinner, he warmly thanked me for making the meal. And when your lanky, six-foot-two teenage son gives you that kind of compliment, it makes you want to cook meatloaf with special glaze every night, if you know what I mean.

While teenagers and thankfulness aren't typically known to go together, I've found that it helps immensely if you start by teaching your child to express thankfulness as early as possible.

Sit down with your son and give him the words to say, helping him with the tone if necessary. Don't wait for him to "feel" thankful, but help him understand that thankfulness is a choice. Then let him know how meaningful his words of gratitude are and that saying thanks isn't a mere formality but truly impacts the other person. Tell him how it brightens your day and makes you want to do more of whatever it was that earned his thank-you. Tell him his expression of thanks blesses you.

I *enjoy* talking with you.

Letting your son know you enjoy talking with him is a simple message he needs to hear. It's another way of saying "I like you" and "I approve of you" and "I think you're a great person."

When they are young, kids seem to chatter nonstop! When they get a little older, the regular back-and-forth communication often tapers off for a variety of reasons, and it can be frustrating as a parent to try to get your tween or teen to talk. Stay positive, stay connected, and continue to mention to your son how you enjoy talking with him. Quality time almost always comes out of quantity time. You can't make him communicate, but you can ensure that he knows you still enjoy talking with him.

And when he does open up, make sure you don't problem-solve, correct, overtalk, or only half listen.

You're older with plenty of life experience and more wisdom, but he didn't come for all that; he just wanted to talk with you. Be sure he knows you like his ideas and value his thoughts—even if you have to bite your tongue!

By staying positive and connected, you keep the door open for when he needs to come to you with something deeper that he's been wrestling with—a serious life challenge.

And he will come; it's just a matter of time before he reaches out for your wisdom and input. He'll want your advice because you value him as a person and always enjoy talking with him.

You've *matured* so much over the past few months.

Most people might not have noticed, the change was so small—nearly imperceptible. And yet, as his mom, I saw our son had been making better choices in a few key areas, such as responding with a better attitude and doing jobs without having to be told.

It seemed as if something had suddenly clicked, and it was encouraging to see. Except that I realized he probably couldn't see it for himself. It's hard to discern your own growth, isn't it? It's not unlike when a child doesn't realize how much taller they've grown until they stand up against a wall, and you make that small pencil mark showing the inches they've gained in the previous months. Then you watch them walk away from the wall, smiling and feeling significantly taller already.

Let your son know that you've watched him make better choices, and tell him what a difference it is making and how much you admire him for it. Point out that he is not only growing taller but also growing in maturity and wisdom.

You have a *sharp* mind.

One terrific way to encourage your son to grow in maturity and think for himself is to help him see that he has a sharp mind, that he's a good thinker and can solve problems and overcome obstacles.

Look for an opportunity when he comes up with an interesting solution to some big challenge—that's his mind at work. Let him know you noticed how he figured it out and came up with the perfect answer. Tell him you're proud of the way he thinks!

Most everything in life will teach a young man that he's average, doesn't measure up, and won't amount to much. But your son has fantastic thoughts, ideas, and plans. And if he has parents who have purposed to notice his best moments in problem-solving, he will grow with confidence in his ability and competence, and then it won't much matter what life has to say. His perspective and self-perception will already be resilient to such discouragement because his parents were there first, speaking the truth into his heart: son, you have a sharp mind!

I *applaud* the way you look out for others.

I never would have known if the other parents hadn't said something. But these friends expressed their gratitude for how our youngest son had impacted their own little guy. As his mother, I wish I could've taken credit, but that hardly seemed right since I wasn't even aware of the incident.

Earlier in the week at school, our young teen had gone over during the lunch hour to play soccer with their five-year-old boy, which made our son seem pretty cool to the boy's classmates.

The other part of the story I didn't know was that previous to this day, their son had been bullied and left out by the others in his class. The kids had looked down on him because he was a little smaller and shyer than the others. But there's nothing like a "cool" teenager giving special attention to a younger child to make him shine—to others and to himself.

I wish I would've had a "big brother" like that when I was in grade school. I could've used an older friend who looked kindly on me. Maybe that's what made me especially glad about that sweet situation with our son and his little friend on the playground.

So encourage your son to look out for others and "catch" the moment when he does. Then tell him what a blessing it is to you and everyone around him.

You stepped up and took *responsibility.* That's what a good man does.

Sometimes things go wrong. Maybe he wasn't thinking in the moment. Perhaps he was careless. Maybe it was a situation entirely out of his control but that happened on his watch. At some point in your son's life, all of these things will come to pass. And that's just it—they pass. Let your son know you won't define him by his mistakes and shortcomings.

At times a parent can come down so hard that the next time something goes sideways, a son won't want to bring it into the light and will avoid responsibility. That's more about you than it is about him. Even if you've made mistakes in the past, today is a new day. Let your son understand that you will never let his mistake define him in your eyes. This approach will embolden him to take more responsibility, and when he does, you'll be ready to point out the good in an otherwise not-so-good situation.

You *inspire* people.

I confess that I was a bit of a nervous mom. What parent isn't when their child is walking up onstage for the end-of-the-year speech contest—his first ever? Then I almost panicked. Where were his notes? He had forgotten to take his notes. Why was he so calm? He didn't seem to care about his notes and started giving his speech without them.

My heart was hitting my chest like a hammer and I held my breath as he began to speak. I wondered just how far he would get, but he never stopped. He never even halted. Unbeknownst to any of us, he had memorized his entire speech. His teacher and classmates clapped kindly and enthusiastically when he was done.

On the way home, we asked, "Why did you decide to memorize your speech?"

"I thought it would be a fun surprise," he said with a "nothing-to-it" grin.

Well, he got that right!

How surprised we were the following year when student after student ascended the stage without notes and gave their speeches from memory. What started out as a fun surprise inspired many to follow suit, creating a new trend for speech night.

Has your son ever done something that went beyond your expectations? Has he ever taken an idea to the next level and encouraged others, by his example, to reach higher? Tell him, "Son, when you do the unexpected, when you surpass expectations, you inspire others to do bigger, better things!"

I *admire* how you demonstrated self-control in that moment.

Learning to govern one's self is critical for maturity and success. The Bible calls self-control a fruit of the Spirit—the unmistakable evidence of the Spirit's presence in your life. How can you encourage your son to grow in self-government—in self-control?

Let the topic of self-control be a ready conversation. Talk to your son about how exercising self-control is about taking responsibility and being in charge of one's future.

Destiny is built on discipline.

As a boy grows and matures, there are moments when he gets things wrong, is selfish, responds poorly, or has a bad attitude. When this happens, of course, a word of correction or admonition is needed, but you can help him to be aware of his inclinations and to grow in self-control. There are also moments, however, when he gets things right and chooses the better path. As a wise parent, be looking for the "win" in everyday situations. Looking for the win means seizing the moment he gets things right and demonstrates self-control.

You'll need to be vigilant, but when you see him rising to the occasion, *make a big deal about it.* Tell him how proud, impressed, happy, and blessed you are to observe him displaying such a significant quality. And tell him how God is pleased as well! Your son will grow in awareness and responsibility by celebrating those moments, and your relationship will flourish.

You have so many
wonderful ideas.

Let's face it. Some kids are simply nonstop idea machines. They're constantly coming up with one after another. These kids aren't easy to shut down or keep up with, because they're always going off on some notion or another, and, honestly, it can be rather exhausting if you're the parent.

And yet this world is a better place with new ideas.

So rather than letting your young Endless Idea Man tire you, allow yourself to view his energy differently. Everything is affected by your perspective and attitude. What once was cause for exhaustion and even annoyance can actually energize you when seen in a different light. Decide you're going to be one of his biggest fans and supporters and see what a difference it makes.

Even if you never end up going with the latest idea and have strong, practical reasons why maybe you should pass on it, your initial response can still be optimistic encouragement. Say things such as "I like that creative idea" or "What an interesting concept" or "I love hearing about your latest brainstorm."

Don't merely tolerate his steady stream of ideas. He's an intelligent, idea-cranking, active-minded kid!

Loudly cheer him on to his next amazing and creative focus. That's a future world-changer you're encouraging!

I *commend* you for being such a hard worker.

Unless they've been parented to hate it, young men actually enjoy work. Until a few years ago, we had a chicken coop with forty laying hens, and as you might know, chickens are incredibly capable of producing far more than eggs. Before too long, there is a man-sized job to be done cleaning the coop. After gathering the three youngest boys (ages five to nine), I spoke to them directly and with respect. "Young men, I've got a job that needs doing, and it's a tough one. You'll have to work like men to complete it today, but I know you can do it. Remember, around here, when you work like a man, you get paid like a man. And good men do excellent work."

They immediately exchanged glances, knowing they would earn serious money. With that, I sent them to shovel the manure out of the coop and cart it to the garden, four hundred feet away.

"Am I being too hard on them?" I asked myself.

Worried they might be getting discouraged, I went out and picked up a shovel about three hours into the job. When my nine-year-old returned from having dumped the wheelbarrow in the garden, he asked, "What are you doing, Dad?"

"Just thought I'd give you a hand. You guys have been at this for hours."

He looked at me, trying to remain respectful, and said, "You told us you would pay us for doing this job, so I don't get why you're here."

Duly reprimanded, I propped the shovel against the side of the coop and smiled all the way back to the house.

They worked for another two hours and then asked me to inspect. "Excellent work. You are becoming fine young men. Men who know how to work and make their father proud. I'm proud of you all. I've got to get back to the house to tell your mother what you've accomplished."

And, yes, they got paid well!

If we embrace our responsibility and get our heads in the game, it doesn't matter where we live. We can focus our young children's minds on learning the joy and value of work and, in the process, teach them self-respect—that pillar of good character that is acquired only through genuine accomplishment.

Remember Adam? From the very beginning, God made man to work. Let's encourage our sons to work hard—and let's affirm it with our words.

You have a creative mind, and I'm *amazed* by what you build.

Do you have a creative genius on your hands? Our son recently completed building a 2,500-piece LEGO space shuttle. He does have a creative mind, and we are often amazed by what he builds. It is important for us to communicate this to him, but there's another level we parents can reach with our creative sons. Certainly express enthusiasm, then ask your son, "How does it work?"

When we asked our son how the shuttle worked, his mind went into NASA instructor mode, and we became transfixed by his detailed explanation of every intricate part. His face beamed a little brighter that day because asking is another way of affirming your interest in him, his world, and what he does. You and I love that from others, and of course your son will love it from you too.

A boy who comes up with endless LEGO creations, imaginative forts, or the most bewildering contraptions can make a lot of messes. As his wise parent, you can remind yourself that this isn't a mess; it's a creation. Even if it doesn't make sense to you or you don't see the point, his creating, building, and dreaming are part of a necessary process!

Do you have a son who loves to build? Get a project and do it together, always letting him build to his heart's content. Not only that, but tell him how impressed you are by his unusual inventions.

You're like a deep river— *calm* but *powerful.* That's what I see in your quiet confidence.

This world is geared toward the flashier presentation, the more aggressive approach. But it's often the quiet, steady one who isn't first noticed who's the real achiever in life. Perhaps you have a son who's always at the front of the pack, and nothing's wrong with that! But if you have a gentler son with a less forward personality, take time to help him see what the world can't necessarily see when he is young—his underlying power, depth, and substance.

Having a quieter personality isn't a liability. It's an asset, because God made him that way for His unique purposes. Your son will find his inner strength and personal confidence first from how he believes you appraise him.

Celebrate his softer personality as a good quality and a great asset in life. So what if he doesn't naturally put himself forward? Good! Jesus said, "Blessed are the meek [not weak but meek—one who is gentle], for they shall inherit the earth" (Matt. 5:5). And let's not forget, Moses was the meekest of all men, but he became the great leader of millions of people through the most trying of circumstances. No, having a gentle spirit isn't about weakness; it's power under control. And God can do great things with that!

I *appreciate* how you show me respect.

We want our sons to respect us, not because it makes us feel good but because God wants this for them. The Bible lays it out clearly in the Ten Commandments: honor your father and your mother (see Exod. 20:12). We're not always right, but we're always mom and dad. For teens, this often becomes an increasingly challenging issue.

Near where we live is a spectacular place on the river that plunges over a precipice and into a deep bowl, affording a twenty-foot-high cliff that is popular for jumping and diving. It's great fun. It's also very dangerous and requires a high degree of precaution. And it's a well-frequented party spot. People have died in those enticing, frigid waters.

When our fourteen- and sixteen-year-old asked if they could go there with a seventeen-year-old friend who drives, but without us, we hesitated. After explaining the dangers and the party scene, we just couldn't agree and said no, they couldn't go. We usually say yes to these kinds of requests, so they were a little caught off guard.

We were bracing for the disappointment, but it never came. They don't always respond positively to a negative answer, but this time they did! They kept a cheerful attitude all afternoon and evening. What a blessing that was, and we didn't withhold our deep appreciation for their honoring spirit.

If a moment like this hasn't happened yet for you and your son, it will. And when he does or says something that communicates respect for you? Don't hesitate to commend him for it!

That took a lot of *courage*.
You are becoming a man!

Around 1775, Samuel Johnson said, "Courage is reckoned the greatest of all virtues; because, unless a man has that virtue, he has no security for preserving any other."[1]

Wise words! Courage is critical. And, of course, you want to raise a courageous, confident son. In life, he will discover many opportunities to step forward or to shrink back.

Some kids are naturally courageous. But even if a child starts out timid, he can grow immensely in bravery—if you lead well.

Most kids don't know what they can do or are capable of. That's why you need to show him, to help him see what he can do. Your steady, confident voice of encouragement will build courage in your son's heart. Again, look for the win. When he shows the slightest bit of confidence, pounce on that moment and don't let it go! Tell him, tell his mom or dad, tell your friends in his presence . . . let everyone know, starting with him, that you are so proud of him.

1. Samuel Johnson, "Quotes on Courage," The Samuel Johnson Sound Bite Page, accessed November 16, 2020, https://www.samueljohnson.com/courage.html.

Son, you could run a small country. Maybe even a large one!

I don't think the little guy was much more than seven years old, but he was clearly quite comfortable taking the leadership role. I watched as he casually and confidently gave orders to all the other church kids who were playing outside after the morning service. Some were even older than he was, yet he didn't seem to notice—or care.

He was clearly the guy in charge.

Then his mother realized what was going on, and I could see she felt embarrassed by his bossy behavior. But I only laughed. Sure, we'd probably have some work to do to help guide his gifting—teach him some diplomacy and other essential people skills. But, honestly, the kid was a born leader. And rather than discouraging this child with these natural abilities, we should encourage him as he develops his natural strengths.

Traits that can be potentially annoying or offensive when your son is seven can turn into something quite wonderful and much needed when he is twenty-seven or fifty-seven. So, go ahead, cheer on your bossy boy! Consider yourself blessed for the privilege of bringing up such a strong leader.

You're going to be *successful* in whatever you choose to do.

Did your son do something good? Did he do something well? Land on it. Point it out and tie it to his future, telling him that he's going to be successful no matter what he chooses to do.

On *Off Camera with Sam Jones*, Sam Elliott tells of his tough, outdoorsman father's response when Sam told him he wanted to be an actor. "My dad died thinking I was a total idiot for wanting to be an actor. . . . I wanted him to be proud of me . . . that's the worst part of it."[1]

It's sad to hear Elliott tell this story. Because his dad was a "man's man," he couldn't see any value in the acting/movie-making world that interested his son. Of course, Elliott went on to become an A-list actor, but that is little compensation for the hole his dad left in his heart.

You may not be interested in acting, hunting, or finding the next unnamed planet, but if those are the things your son is interested in or pursuing, don't miss the moment to validate your son's dreams and ideas with your approval.

Focusing on his microsuccesses, based on facts and not false praise, will encourage his belief in his gifting and steer him toward a positive future as he continues to build his character.

1. Sam Elliott, "Where Sam Elliott Learned to Be a Man," YouTube video, 1:32, posted by "theoffcamerashow," June 11, 2017, https://www.youtube.com/watch?v=GGHFYGl6q_M.

By establishing the baseline through the repeated messaging "You will be a success," you're building the firm foundation for how he will come to view himself.

Every young child who believes in himself had a parent who believed in him first.

I *respect* that you are your own man who's not swayed by the crowd.

Sometimes it's easier to make good choices regarding bigger issues. He won't watch that hot new movie with a bad reputation or get caught up with the questionable crowd that's up to no good. But it's the little stuff that can be a real challenge—things like laughing along with others over a joke at someone else's expense. Or going with the popular opinion, even if it's contrary to his conscience.

Standing apart from the crowd in relatively small moments can be the real test.

Is your young man willing to do the hard thing and take a stand? Or does he at least step away from what others are doing or saying when he knows it's not right? Does he avoid making a fuss over it but shun those things that are unkind, unjust, or immoral?

If so, he should be commended. Maybe it's something relatively inconsequential this time, but such brave decisions prepare him for making even bigger ones as he gets older. Let him know you admire his willingness to stand apart.

Wow! Look at those strong muscles!

Boys want to be strong. They want to be capable and competent, and they desire for others to see them as such. Maybe your son handled a demanding job that required muscles. Maybe he helped get the new dishwasher into the utility room. Perhaps he did manual labor until he glistened with sweat. His strength is a big help around the house. Don't be reluctant to let your son know you notice his growing strength. Proverbs 20:29 says, "The glory of young men is their strength."

There's a difference between feeding vanity and pride and recognizing the growing strength of your young man. God made him strong for a reason—to fulfill his calling in life.

I'm grateful for your *determination* to protect those in danger.

I couldn't get the story out of my head. I found myself going over and over it again in my mind, especially knowing it was a true story. One of my favorite Christian authors, who worked as a doctor in Africa many years ago, shared how she was captured and taken by rebel soldiers.

One of the soldiers grabbed her and put a gun to her head, clearly intending severe harm. But one of the village's young teenage boys stepped in between the soldier and her, fully aware of what it would cost him. And, sure enough, right before her horrified eyes, the soldier beat and kicked the boy senseless. Then the soldier went ahead and did what he'd set out to do in the first place against the helpless woman.

That young man must have known he wouldn't be able to stop the soldier and his wicked intentions but later said (though he never fully recovered) there was no way he could simply do nothing and had to try something.

As I shared this compelling story with my church family one Sunday morning, I looked out and caught the eye of one of the young men there—the teenage son of longtime family friends—and I stopped for a moment. Then I added, "And I know this guy would do the same thing for me if we were ever in a similar situation." He nodded gravely in agreement. It was apparent he'd already been rehearsing in his mind how it would've played out if we had been in that awful place.

I was too choked up for a minute to continue with the story, struck by such a strong and sacrificial commitment by one so young. I'm thankful for my young friend and other men like him who are willing to give so much for the people they care about, even at the risk of their lives.

If your son is a hero in the making, tell him how thankful you are for his desire to protect those in harm's way.

I *like* spending time with you.

Parents love their kids—it's a bit of a cliché, but it's also true. The trouble is, parents often don't communicate this fact in a way that is meaningful to their children. Many kids know their parents basically love them and will look after them, but many are left wondering, *Does Dad or Mom actually like me?*

As a parent, you're always speaking powerfully by what you say and what you *do not* say.

A young man gets his first impression of how the world views him from his parents. No matter how young or old your son is, look into his eyes and say, "Son, I like spending time with you. I enjoy being with you." Then follow up that statement by inviting him into your world to be by your side. Show him—prove to him—you appreciate him as a person.

You are *polite*. I really appreciate that.

Seems we often have a crew of boys at our house. It's probably inevitable when you have three teenage sons—and a big-screen television. Plus, we do what we can to make sure there's something hearty for dinner and junk food in the pantry (#dontjudge). And so the guys stream in, grab a bite, and head upstairs to the recreation room for movies and video games (I wanted to add "deep conversation" somewhere in there, but I'm trying to keep it real).

One young man in particular always—and I mean always—makes it a point to thank me for dinner and for having him over. And I never get tired of hearing it from him. He's so polite and thoughtful that I'd welcome him into our home anytime. And I can't help but think of his parents, who taught him such good manners. I'm thankful for them too.

Manners. Those seemingly small details, such as saying thank you and please, waiting for another person, firmly shaking hands, and holding clear eye contact. Do these things really matter all that much?

You know they do.

Manners are yet another important part of communicating respect and care for another person. And everyone is always grateful for a young gentleman in the making. I know that I sure am.

Encourage good manners in your son. Yes, it can be a bit of an uphill climb, but he will thank you (ever so politely) later!

You are *very good* at figuring things out.

There will be a moment when your son is working something out and coming to a conclusion. Maybe he's solved a challenging problem; maybe he's shared his opinion about something—whatever it is, commend him on his intelligence. Let him know you recognize that he is a good thinker!

I can already hear someone saying, "You'll just make him prideful and give him a big head." Yes, this can happen if there is no encouragement to be humble in his training/discipleship. But your son needs to hear that he has a good head on his shoulders. It's a message he's not likely to get in this world, increasingly so for Christian kids who have been taught that God's Word is true.

You're proud of how his mind works. You respect how he thinks about things. Let him know!

Although it's a difficult challenge, I'm *convinced* you can figure it out.

Cleaning out and organizing the garage is no one's ideal job. I find it to be an intimidating task, and I'm a full-grown woman! But Matt had assigned one of our sons the role and was confident he could handle it.

As soon as Matt left for work, however, our son looked to me. He thought maybe we could tackle it together. And we could, except that I wasn't going to figure out this job for him. Instead of him working for me, I told him I would work for him. So, where did he want me to begin?

His eyes swept across the crowded, messy garage, and he let out a small sigh (I know the feeling). Then he decided we'd start with the boxes on the floor.

It's true that if the job had been up to me, I would have suggested starting with those ugly piles in the corner, but it was on him this time. So we did it his way. And as we went along that day, I saw him gain momentum and grow increasingly confident.

Don't be too quick to solve things for your son. You're building confidence by giving him space and encouraging him to work it out. Communicate to him that you're behind him and positive he has what it takes to figure out what needs to be done.

The Good Book says a man skilled in his work will *stand* before kings. That makes me think of you.

Has your son mastered a skill? Is he accomplished in a given area? It's encouraging to him when you connect that achievement with something the Word says about his shining future. It's just another way of telling him you believe in him and in his destiny. In such situations, I like to say to my boys, "Proverbs 22:29 says, 'A man skillful in his work . . . will stand before kings,' but, in your case, you'll probably be a king!"

Excellence is achieved only through diligence. When you see this process unfolding in your son's life and he gains mastery of a skill, remind him of where, according to King Solomon, such achievement takes a young man.

You're *loyal* to those you love.

I should tell you straight out that we were in the wrong.

His dad and I had made a few offhand "evaluative" comments about one of our son's friends. We had some (possibly) legitimate concerns and casually mentioned these criticisms in a passing conversation.

But after we had done so, we noticed the troubled expression on our son's face. Although he is rarely ruffled by much, he was clearly annoyed by what we'd said about his friend and immediately came to his defense.

"I wish you wouldn't talk that way about my friend. He's a really great guy, and I don't think you're being fair!"

Although we were a bit surprised by the fierceness of his response, we received the rebuke. We hadn't meant to be unkind, but we certainly could've been more charitable, so we offered an apology right then and there. Then we told him how much we appreciated how fiercely loyal he was to the people he cared about, and we were glad he was that way.

Commend your son for his strong sense of loyalty; it's a terrific quality in a young man.

It's not easy
to *conquer* your fear,
but you did it.

It was a blisteringly hot day in Central Oregon. We have many of those in the summer, and we always have a ready answer for how to cool off: *Let's go to the lake!* This particular day, I had something specific in mind. On a previous outing, one of our sons had stood on a rock above the water and wanted to jump in but couldn't quite make himself do it. I didn't push.

When your son is in the process of finding his courage, it's a delicate balance of your encouraging and believing, but not pushing. I could see in his eyes as we set up our towels and the awning that he really wanted to jump. As everyone got busy sunbathing or swimming, he walked over to the precipice and stood, looking down into the water as if he were eyeing the abyss.

"Hey, sonny," I called, "you can do it!"

He stepped back, then forward, peering into the water. He stood there for the longest time and then he turned back, only to turn again, run, and jump off.

My heart just about burst out of my chest. We were all so proud of him. We cheered like fans at an NFL playoff game after the winning touchdown. It was awesome. That first jump is so hard sometimes, isn't it? Then he must have jumped off that rock a hundred times before we headed home.

In a quiet moment, I took him aside and said, "It's not easy to conquer your fear, but you did it!"

It may not involve jumping off a rock into a body of water, but a time like this is coming in your son's life. Be ready to affirm him in conquering his fears and in his growing manhood.

I have *complete* trust in you.

"Do you know why I call on you so often?" I asked our middle son. He smiled at my question, which told me he had actually noticed that I do call on him often. But he also admitted he didn't know why.

So I explained it to him. I told him how much I appreciated his reliability and follow-through. And the reason I called out his name the most was because I had confidence that he could be trusted with the job or the information. A rare find these days.

He beamed brightly when he heard that.

But our conversation didn't stop there. I wanted him to see that this wasn't only about the present; it was also about the future. It was about preparing him for the kind of husband he will be: trustworthy. The kind of friend he will be: trustworthy. And the kind of work he will do someday: trustworthy.

You can help your son become someone people can trust by speaking into his life now. Let him know how meaningful it is that you can depend on him, and affirm his dependability.

You ask such
great questions.

Has your son ever asked you a question when you've been pre-occupied with something else? In times like those, nothing's easier than brushing him off. After all, you're focused and concentrating on your priority. You might say, "This isn't a good time! Can't your question wait?" Or how about that question that seems stupid or a little goofy? It's tempting to answer in a belittling way, isn't it? After all, he should have been able to figure it out himself, right?

If you have reacted this way in the past, it's time to change. It's time to understand something super important: a question from your son is *wonderful!* It doesn't matter what you thought about the substance of his query; you're older, with a lot more life experience. If you want to encourage communication and openness, you're going to have to give positive input when he does venture a question.

Affirm who he is by affirming the questions he asks.

I can see you're *choosing* to be strong.

Feelings can be powerful, but they're also like fickle friends—completely unreliable and constantly changing. We need to encourage our sons not to be victims of how they feel.

This isn't a statement about denying legitimate feelings. It's about properly appraising them and responding appropriately. A son driven by his feelings will be reckless.

Teaching your son to be in command of his feelings starts in the physical realm. When the parent of a young son sees him skin his knee and then acts as if the child is bleeding from his carotid artery, it's no surprise that the little boy responds in kind. Overreacting does not help.

While we always want to be compassionate, caring parents when our son is in pain, we also want to lovingly help him manage hard things and hurts without complaining or making an overly big deal about them. That toughness we want to instill starts by our showing our sons how we admire their strength and endurance when faced with an "owie" or fall when they are young.

You're a real *go-getter*!

Go-getters come in all shapes and sizes. By the time our oldest (now twenty-seven) was almost sixteen, he had held many airsoft wars at Stonyfield, our ten-acre pile of rocks in the country—think General Patton! Then he had an idea. Why not create an airsoft association where serious airsofters could achieve different levels of badges? Before long, he had dads and sons coming to his epic wars, with Stonyfield converted into a battle zone, replete with hideouts, barricades, and recon stations. He named it Central Oregon Airsoft Association.

Son, you're a real go-getter!

Then we have another son, our sixth child, who is eight years younger. He's quiet, unassuming, and rarely puts himself forward. These two boys couldn't be more different. And yet every time something is happening—a mountain bike ride, Ultimate Frisbee, or a movie night with friends—wherever there is a whir of activity, look into it and it's our quiet sixth child who's moving behind the scene, networking with everyone to make it all happen.

Son, you're a real go-getter!

In both cases, our sons grew into their skill sets, based on their very different personalities, but the message we send to both is the same. Is your son young and beginning to show initiative in something? Your messaging—the way you frame your perception of what he is doing—will encourage him to see his growing competence and ability.

Through your words and actions, you provide your son's first perspective and understanding of who he is. If he's very young and chasing a bug in the garage until he catches it or older and pursuing more mature endeavors—wherever he is on the age spectrum, help him see himself as a man of action, purpose, and drive.

Son, you're a real go-getter!

I'm *fascinated* by how resourceful you are.

Maybe your son made a boat out of an old milk jug, or perhaps he found a way to do his chores faster. Or maybe he's a Tom Sawyer, organizing and motivating others to get work done. Whatever it is, when his resourcefulness shows itself, commend him for it— even in small matters.

In Luke 16, Jesus told a parable (an earthly story with a heavenly meaning) about an unjust steward who was about to be fired. Before the fateful day, the steward worked hard to make many deals with his boss's debtors that he might have their favor when he was sent packing. When his boss discovered what he had done, he was commended for being wise. Now, that's resourceful!

To be resourceful is to figure out a way to achieve an objective when conventional or obvious methods are unavailable. Life presents many situations where resourcefulness is needed. To effectively navigate life, a child will need to learn resourcefulness. Some kids are more inclined, some less, to be resourceful, but every child can grow in this area. Look for opportunities to commend his ingenuity. A word of affirmation from you brings a light heart and an increasingly keen focus on tackling the next challenge!

Life brings many battles, but you can *count on me* to have your back.

Battles big and small are coming your son's way. Before he finds himself in the midst of the next battle, he needs to hear something from you. He needs to know you will be right there with him—that you always have his back.

In various ways, life has a way of making us feel alone against the world. You've felt that as an adult, haven't you? Let your son know that will never happen to him. No matter what the day holds, you're right there by his side, every step of the way.

I am so *pleased* with you.

Growing up, I knew my parents were proud of me. Even if they didn't say it in so many words, I believed they were proud of who I was as a good student and a relatively responsible child.

And perhaps you're proud of your son too.

But even more than knowing my parents were proud of my accomplishments or character traits, I wanted to know they were pleased with me. I longed to see that they took delight in me and who I was as a person—that even if I had more growing to do (and I most certainly did), they were thoroughly satisfied with me as I was right then.

As a parent, we can be so committed to correcting and helping our children grow that we forget to communicate that we're *pleased* with them. The sad truth is that most kids sense disapproval from their parents—whether mistakenly or not.

So be clear with your son. Don't leave any room for doubt. Tell him straight-out how pleased you are with who he is as a person.

You showed real patience, a *fine quality* in a young man.

Boys are not typically known for their patience, and, in many cases, they're just mimicking mom and dad. Adults often justify their impatience because of the intensity of the moment. Is it any wonder our kids aren't patient?

Even so, patience is not a quality natural to our flesh, young or old. We want what we want—when we want it! But to love well in marriage and parenting and life, patience is not optional; it's required. First Corinthians 13:4 says, "Love is patient." You're a discipler. How are you doing in discipling your son in patience through your behavior?

Without patience, loving well is not possible. There's also another reason patience is essential. In Galatians 5:22–23, we discover that patience is evidence (fruit) of the Spirit in one's life—it's proof we are walking in the Spirit and not in our flesh. Patience needs to be present in our own lives so we can effectively teach it to our kids.

Patience really is an amazing quality in the life of a young man. When you see it, be sure to point it out and affirm it. Remind him that he's not only blessing others, but he's also pleasing God.

Son, you're such a *handsome* young man.

Maybe you're surprised we'd include this one. It's possible you find it unnecessary or a little light for an affirmation. But let me tell you a story that might make you change your mind.

One day many years into our marriage, I walked by my husband and remarked what a handsome guy he was. I thought he'd appreciate the compliment, but it turned out to be so much more than that.

He paused, then went on to tell me how, as a young eleven-year-old, he believed himself to be so ugly—even though he was a perfectly good-looking kid—that he went through all the family photo albums and tore out every picture of himself. You can see his entire family standing in front of the Christmas tree or sitting around the dining table—everyone is visible, except for one young boy whose picture was ripped out.

This nearly broke my heart. To think there was a young lad who had such an awful (and mistaken) appraisal of his appearance! So you can't be surprised that I make sure our sons know I consider them quite handsome, thank you very much!

And I hope you do the same with yours.

I can see you're growing *Strong* on the inside.

Our sons must come to understand the connection between making choices and the life they are building—that they must govern themselves or they will be governed by others.

Coming to self-awareness of the choices one is making is a critical milepost on the road to maturity. The hardest decisions are those that go against one's natural inclinations—a child choosing between the larger and smaller cookie, a teenager sticking to a commitment to a friend although an enticing option just presented itself, an older young man deciding between self-indulgence and self-sacrifice. Whenever such a moment presents itself (whether great or small) and your son chooses against self-interest and for self-sacrifice, be sure to commend him. He's growing strong inside.

Whoever you marry is going to be one *lucky* woman.

Most young men want to get married someday. What kind of husband will your son be? You have a powerful voice in helping him think about those future days by highlighting his best moments at home now.

When heading out to the lake, our son asks himself, "What would Mom want me to pack for her?" Another son makes me coffee almost every morning. They're thoughtful and considerate young men. They're also normal boys, so they don't get it right every time. But when they do act in a way that puts me or their sisters first, they're showing the kinds of husbands they will be.

Capture that moment with a positive affirmation about the woman they will marry someday. Tell them that based on how they acted in that moment, she's going to be one blessed lady! Be on the watch for the thoughtful things he says or does, and when appropriate, let him know you believe his future bride will be getting a real gem.

You are very different from me, but that's a *good thing*, and I love your unique personality.

With eight children, we were bound to have some who are similar to us and some who are very different! And, yes, it has a major impact on how we relate to each other. It's important not only to consider those differences when communicating but to celebrate them, principally because your son is a unique, wonderful young man created in God's image. Is he vastly different from you? Good! That's how God made and gifted him.

It's not uncommon to view different as not quite right or outright wrong, which, of course, is ridiculous. Are you the strong, bold, forward type and he the shy, quiet, reserved type—or vice versa? Either way, both when he's young and when he's older, he needs to hear your approval of his personhood—his wonderful, different way of thinking and being.

One day he will climb life's mountains, and the feat will be all the more attainable because he was valued during his exploring years as he tried to determine which mountain he would scale.

Thank you for taking care of that with a *cheerful* spirit.

Matt decided it was our one son's job to take out the kitchen trash. It was a small responsibility in reality, but you would've thought we were asking him to take the garbage out to the moon rather than the trash bin only some ten yards from our front door.

Our son did what he was asked to do.

But the slow, heavy walk and the burdened sighs that accompanied the task made it such an unpleasant experience that I would have vastly preferred to do the job myself. I told my husband that I'd rather carry the trash out every day of the week than have to deal with our son's bad attitude.

Oh, our son knew better than to loudly complain, but there were other equally effective ways of communicating his displeasure, so he made the chore miserable for both of us. And I took it personally.

But then one day I stopped him midway to the moon (aka our garbage bin) and asked him, "Do you know how hard you're making this—not only for yourself but for *me*? The Bible says, 'Whatever you do, work heartily, as for the Lord and not for men' [Col. 3:23]. Is that what you're doing?"

He seemed surprised, as if he'd never thought about it like that. I explained that I didn't want a job done nearly as much as I wanted a cheerful attitude about it. Apparently this was an eye-opening conversation for him.

Most kids spend zero time considering how they affect other people—and probably especially their parents—so be sure to teach your son to understand the impact his attitude has on you and what God's Word says about work. Then let him know you appreciate the improved attitude as much as the task accomplished!

You're not weak; you have the *power* to make right choices.

Before your son has given his life to Christ and received God's free gift of grace, he can do things that are understood by him and others to be good, but he can do nothing to commend himself to God. And he can never triumph over sin. But when he is reconciled to God through Jesus Christ, everything changes.

Second Corinthians 5:17 says, "Therefore, if anyone is in Christ, he is a new creation. The old has passed away; behold, the new has come."

What are those new things?

1. *He has been given POWER.* According to 2 Timothy 1:7, "God has not given us a spirit of fear, but of power and of love and of a sound mind" (NKJV). Help your son see that he is not weak. He is strong because he has been given the Spirit of power. He is indwelt by the Spirit of power.

2. *He has been given PROTECTION.* Your son may be in a battle to choose right from wrong, but he has been given protection for the battle! Ephesians 6:10–18 says he has been given armor for the wars he will wage, and he's been given a sword for the fight!

3. *He has been given PROVISION to win every battle to triumph over every temptation.* First Corinthians 10:13 says, "There hath no temptation taken you but such as is common to man: but God is faithful, who will not suffer you to be tempted above that ye are able; but will with the temptation also make a way to escape, that ye may be able to bear it" (KJV).

The Scriptures are powerful, but only if we believe them. If we believe wrong, we'll never live strong. We must trust what God has said and not base our reality on what we feel.

Help your son see that he is not weak. He is strong in the Spirit. He's been given *power*, *protection*, and *provision*. And God has his back!

I *believe* you can do it!

Our youngest son was in that awkward in-between stage: no longer a little boy but not quite ready to run with the big kids. Here our family was prepared to ride the sand dunes for the day as part of our summer family vacation. Matt and I were taking our youngest daughter with us in the dune buggy, while the rest of the kids wanted to ride their own quads.

Our youngest son hated the idea of being a mere passenger tagging along with the "old folks," but he wasn't too confident in driving his own machine either. I could see him wrestling with the options in his mind. Play it safe and go with us or gulp down his fear and venture out on his own?

"You can do this, son. I know you can," I whispered in his ear so the others couldn't hear. "Even though you've never done this before, I'm sure you'll figure it out in no time."

He didn't answer me but stared silently at the bright red four-wheeler, wanting so badly to ride out like his older siblings but doubting he had what it took to do so. Then after several minutes of deliberation, he made up his mind. He walked over to the ATV and asked the instructor to show him how it worked.

Although he started out slowly, before long, he was keeping up with the pack and riding the dunes like he'd been doing it all his life. Oh, and if you could've only seen his big smile!

Sometimes what your son needs is just a little push to encourage him to take that step. Let him know you believe in him. Communicate that you're confident in his abilities, and then watch him fly.

When you acted in that way, you demonstrated *genuine* leadership.

Years ago, we met with a large group of parents at the park. Then he showed up: Mr. Type-A, Hard-Driving Personality. His timid son followed close behind. "C'mon, son, catch up. Be a leader!" He must have used that phrase a hundred times: "Be a leader! Be a leader!" The little lad looked like he'd be happier practicing the oboe by himself.

We mustn't fulfill our own desires in attempting to live vicariously through our children. Relentlessly pushing our children never redounds to their benefit and will eventually push them away.

Most parents want their kids to be leaders, and in virtually every child's life, at some point situations arise that allow them to show initiative and leadership. Leadership can be exercised in many ways, and quiet leadership is often overlooked. In keeping with his gifting, inform your child's self-perception by landing on the moments that bring out the leader in him. Some kids were born natural leaders. Others take a softer, gentler approach, but that doesn't mean they will be any less effective in life. Embrace him for who he is.

You worked hard until the job was done. *Impressive!*

The message came as quite a surprise. This young family we knew sent a simple text telling us they were on their way to help us with our yard work. What an incredible and encouraging gift.

Our own family had been through a difficult season of sickness and various trials, so they were coming over to cheer us up with some extra hands. And cheer us up it did.

Their entire family, including their two-year-old son, got right to work weeding and clearing the neglected flower beds. After a while, the littlest one became bored and wandered off to play, soon followed by his four-year-old sister.

That left their six-year-old son to keep on by himself. I could tell he was growing hot and tired, but his dad gently urged him to keep after the job. And so he kept pulling up the seemingly endless jungle of weeds until, at last, he finished his assigned task.

Then his dad just as quietly complimented him: "Good job, son! You worked until the task was finished."

He wasn't even my son and I was bursting with pride (the right kind) at his perseverance and diligence. I could already see what an impact this kind of training—and recognition—would have on this young man's life in the years to come.

Anyone can start a job, but staying with it is rare. Encourage your son to keep on, and then be sure to applaud a job well done.

You are as *bold* as a lion.

To a very high degree, a son sees himself through the eyes and words of his parents. What he hears indirectly, along with what is said directly to him, will inform how he views himself.

Building up boldness in the heart of your son looks different from son to son. One little boy will dive into life headfirst without a thought, while the other will take a more cautious approach. What kind of personality does your son have? This is important to understand as you seek to build up a bold but wise spirit in your son.

The process can begin at a very young age. If your son discovers frogs or lizards for the first time and is willing to hold one, tell him, "Son, you are as bold as a lion!" If he is in his teens and is ready to approach a challenging situation head-on, tell him the same thing, "Son, you are as bold as a lion! I'm so proud of you!"

If you see him with the boldness of a lion—an image he is sure to love applied to him—he will begin to appraise himself the same way. For most young kids, building boldness is an incremental process and can be started with the simplest moments of triumph. Keep an eye out for the next moment you can speak boldness into your son's heart.

God knows the number of hairs on your head. He sees you and has a plan for your *best life*.

Our one son seemed a little lost that summer. We could see he was discouraged and rather lonely too. As his parents, we did what we could to cheer him up, but it wasn't enough.

Due to a conspiring set of circumstances, he found himself with almost no friends his age and not much to look forward to. Our hearts ached for him. He's a good kid and a joy to be around, but that didn't help with how he felt. From his perspective, everyone else appeared to be enjoying friends, doing things, and going places. And all our "Don't worry, your time will come" assurances did little to comfort him.

He said he felt invisible.

And that was our chance to tell him the truth: God sees him and cares immensely about every detail of his life—including how he was feeling right then. God sees and has the perfect plan in place, made just for him!

There might come a day when your son will wonder if God actually cares about him. He will feel so small and insignificant that it won't seem possible that our heavenly Father could notice him, let alone look after him.

This is your chance to tell him that the Bible says God knows the very number of hairs on his head: "Why, even the hairs of your head are all numbered. Fear not; you are of more value than many sparrows" (Luke 12:7).

So remind your son that God is always near and ever mindful of him. He has a God who loves and watches over him—down to the very last detail.

You see what needs to be done and *do it* without being asked.

When our sons first start taking responsibility, we might be inclined to focus on the wrong things.

One summer day, our family was headed out on a camping trip. Naturally, Lisa and I had too many things to get done before we left, let alone pack. But one of our sons took it upon himself to "do it all!" You could see his single-minded focus as he walked from the house to the truck to the shed to the garage, getting everything together and loading the pickup.

Awesome! It was just awesome to see him work as I focused on what I needed to do. Then it was time to go, and I walked out to the truck to look things over. Immediately, I could see that he had loaded everything differently than I would have. Without really thinking, I began to speak . . . then caught myself. This wasn't the time for evaluation, assessment, and instruction. It was the time for unmitigated praise! He took the initiative and worked until the job was complete—all without me saying a word or lifting a finger.

If your son takes initiative, focus on that and let him know you are confident in the future that awaits him. Then, sometime later, maybe a *long time* later, you can offer your wise suggestions.

Just praise his initiative, and you'll find he'll be scouting additional opportunities to be a self-starter.

I like the way you notice and care for those who could use a *little extra love*.

Our youngest daughter is often overlooked. It is not that anyone means to pass her by, but many don't know what to say or what to do for a girl who has severe special needs and is confined to a wheelchair. Because it makes people feel generally uncomfortable or uncertain, they tend to do nothing at all. They will only vaguely smile and walk on by her. And to be totally truthful, it hurts her heart—all our hearts.

And that is what makes this one young man stand out all the more. He's a friend of our boys and often pops by the house for food, fun, and games. But before heading upstairs to join the festivities, I often find him "deep" in conversation with our special girl. He asks her all the standard questions, like how her day went or what she's been up to lately. And you should see the way her face beams with pleasure at his attention! She will then talk his ears off (she's quite the chatterbox!), and he listens as if he can't imagine anything more interesting than what she has to say.

This young man has no idea what his care means to us or how many times he's made us tear up with his kind attention toward her.

And I don't know what his parents did to make him so tender toward the "poor and needy," but they've sure raised up a son who is a blessing to many—but especially to those of us who have a special one who could use some extra love and attention.

I hope you too will encourage your young man, no matter his age, to be mindful of those around him who might be wanting a little tender loving care.

You're sure looking *Sharp* today.

My dad was a proud veteran—a radio operator for the Naval Air Force during the Korean War. So you probably know what kind of a haircut I had for the first thirteen years of my life: *high and tight*—military crew cut, all the way! Then we moved to Canada in 1970, and the sixties had had a big impact on everything, including boys' hairstyles. I badgered Dad to let me grow my hair long until I wore him down. I was already pretty scruffy, and before long, an Old English sheepdog had nothing on me!

Boys often specialize in looking scruffy. Don't worry. Relax. It's not a big deal. It will pass (when I went off to boarding school, I started taking showers and mopped up pretty well). In the meantime, don't make negative comments about his appearance. A time will come when looking sharp and sprucing up will matter more. When that happens, it's your moment to commend him for how fine he looks. What matters now is that he knows you think he's great and doesn't have to be a certain way to be approved of and liked by you.

You demonstrated an *obedient* heart when you responded that way.

My friend and I were having the most delightful conversation in our front room when she realized why her four-year-old son had been so quiet. He had discovered a piece of glass décor, which, for whatever boyish reason, had wholly captured his imagination. He turned it into a rocket ship, then some kind of medieval weapon, and so on. I never knew one glass candleholder could be so versatile. Anyway, he was having a grand old time with the fragile piece of glass until his mother called him over and asked him to hand it to her.

He stared at his mom with obvious incredulity that she'd ask him to give up something so precious and entertaining. She repeated her request. His strong reluctance to comply was evident to us both. But he finally, slowly, painfully released his grasp and gave it to her.

After he ran off, his mother began to apologize to me. "I'm sorry. We're working on first-time obedience, but . . ." And her sentence trailed off with a note of discouragement.

And then I offered her my perspective on the situation. Yes, I observed the hesitant obedience, but I also saw that her son had ultimately chosen to give over his newfound "toy"—even when he was loath to do so. You could visibly see her little guy wrestling to overcome his desire to keep what he wanted so badly in order to choose what was right.

I believe her young son demonstrated surprisingly strong

character in making the right choice—small delay or not—and was to be commended for it.

If you have a young son or perhaps an older son, don't hold back when he ultimately makes that hard but right choice—even if there is a bit of wrestling before he gets there.

You are *highly* capable, and that's why I depend on you to do it well.

A regular part of growing up as a Jacobson kid is that I (Dad) tell you what needs to be done—and expect you to figure it out.

Just last week, I purchased a new faucet for the boys' bathroom. I set it on the counter and asked my sixteen-year-old son to install it.

"But I've never done this before," he said. To which I replied, "I know, but I'm confident you can do it!"

Every new skill seems like rocket science until you are faced with the challenge of digging in and figuring it out. Tell your son you are confident in him. You know he is highly capable and intelligent. When you take his abilities seriously, he will start to believe in himself and do the same.

A few wins in this column, and he'll be ready to assemble a space shuttle!

You stood for the truth, *regardless* of the consequences. That's what good men do.

Although we suspected some bullying was going on, this particular teenage bully was the sneaky type and tended to do his worst when no one was looking. What made it harder was that the bully also happened to be a church kid and had it out for the pastor's son—who, in this case, was our oldest son.

One day the church bully got his brother to gang up with him against our son and "jump" him when no one else was around. It quickly turned into an old-fashioned fistfight with two against one, but our son held his own. Eventually, someone discovered the tussle and broke it up.

Naturally, the bully quickly concocted a big story that made him look like the victim rather than the instigator. He was a convincing storyteller, and his dad was all too ready to believe his tale. It looked like the kid was going to get away with yet another incident—until our son stood up to both the bully and his brother and bravely declared, "You're a liar." And he wouldn't back down.

This wasn't the last incident with this particular kid, but it was the beginning of putting a stop to his cowardly meanness. Sometimes it takes someone who is brave enough to speak the truth—no matter the consequences—and the world will be all the better for it.

Encourage your own young man that although it might cost him to stick to the truth, he's making the right choice.

Thank you for listening to our advice. That means you're *growing* in wisdom.

Kids don't have to be too old before they learn that their parents aren't perfect. We make mistakes, don't we? A parent doesn't always give wise advice, but it's always wise for a child to listen to his dad's and mom's counsel. This is a major theme in the book of Proverbs.

In Proverbs 1:8–9, Solomon writes,

> My son, hear the instruction of your father,
> And do not forsake the law of your mother;
> For they will be a graceful ornament on your head,
> And chains about your neck. (NKJV)

King Solomon advises every son to listen to his parents!

We encourage our children to read the book of Proverbs. It's a great place to start. There are thirty-one chapters—perfect for one a day! We even had our kids write a few verses in a journal as part of their daily writing practice. King Solomon, the wisest man who ever lived, urges children to listen to their parents' voices and heed their advice.

When your son listens and takes your counsel, point out the wisdom of not forging ahead alone. Let him hear your commendation.

Your dad and mom will *always* stand with you.

While I believe our intentions were good, here's an area that Matt and I wish we could do over with our older kids. We thought we should be evenhanded when it came to our kids and their conflicts with others. If an issue arose between our kid and another child, or even with an adult, we did our best to approach the situation with impartiality.

We were well-intentioned . . . but we were wrong.

Oh, not that we should turn a blind eye to our kids' faults or misdeeds. But in our attempts to be fair-minded, we inadvertently communicated to our children that we weren't necessarily standing by them—and they desperately needed to know we would always be on their side, no matter what.

After careful reflection and more than a few regrets, we concluded that we don't want our children to ever worry or wonder about whose side we're on. Yes, it's good to be wise and fair, but when it comes to our kids, you can count on us standing with them every time.

I hope you won't make the same mistake we did. Tell your son, loud and clear, that you'll always stand with him—in good times and bad, in best moments or in messes and mistakes.

I am your *biggest* fan.

It's easy and natural to celebrate your child's wins with other people. And that's great—but not as good as it could be. Your son needs to hear that you are his biggest fan. This is a positive affirmation for just about any win. Did he get a good score on a school paper? Did he win an award? Did he do something kind for someone else? Did he show his great sense of humor and crack a hilarious joke? Did he stand up to a bully? Whatever he did, tell him, "I'm your biggest fan!"

Celebrate your son's wins with *him*, not just with other people.

You took on that big responsibility and *performed* well.

I came into the kitchen and, although I could hear noises, I couldn't see anything or anyone. Finally, I walked to the other side of the kitchen island to see our youngest son lying on the floor with his head under the sink. He had cleared out all the junk from the cabinet beneath the sink so that he could squeeze his teenage body into the relatively small space. I carefully stepped over the various tools spread out across the kitchen tile.

"Whatchya doing down there, son?"

"Fixing your sink, Mom."

I hope I didn't look as shocked as I felt, but honestly, I'd never seen the kid doing any kind of plumbing work. It was slightly risky, if you asked me. I went to find his father to find out why our thirteen-year-old was suddenly now our new plumber. He laughed at my concern and replied that when our son had found out that it would be two hundred dollars (*two hundred!*) to get a new faucet, he wanted to try his hand at fixing the old one.

Right. For that kind of money, I was game to see what the boy could do. And wouldn't you know it, less than thirty minutes later, he sauntered over to inform me, "Well, Mom, I just saved you two hundred bucks!" He'd done it. He'd found the problem, and the faucet was working again.

Legitimately impressed, I told him how proud and thankful I was for the job he'd done. And we both learned something new about him that day.

Let your son take on those bigger-than-him tasks and then applaud him when he gets them done.

I'm *super* impressed to see you working so diligently at your studies.

Much of what your son does today isn't about today; it's about tomorrow. When a bricklayer is building a house in the heat of the day, it's not about the immediate experience, it's about what each incremental step he's taking will ultimately produce.

Has your son worked diligently on his studies? Has he developed a strong work ethic? This is all too rare these days and worthy of your strong commendation. It's encouraging to him that you notice his diligence.

It's also vital for you to connect the dots for him between the hard work he's doing now that doesn't seem too important and the habits he has developed that will propel him forward toward God's best plans for him.

You're a man of your word. That means people will *trust* what you say.

I couldn't understand why he was putting his coat back on. He'd just returned home exhausted from a long day of work, the kind that ended up going hours longer than expected. It didn't make any sense for him to be heading back out the door after he'd had a quick bite to eat.

"Sorry, Mom, but I told Grandpa I'd come over to help him after work, so I have to go."

I tried to stop him, telling him that his grandpa would understand once he heard the circumstances. But it didn't make any difference, and back out he went.

I sat quietly at the kitchen table for several minutes after he'd gone, full of conflicting emotions. My mother's heart was concerned that he was overdoing it. But his dad said he was proud of our young man, and he'd done the right thing by keeping his word, reminding me that he'd have harder decisions than this to make when he grew older.

And in my heart, I knew what his dad had said was true.

Plenty of people would say he didn't have to go, to keep his word in that instance, or it wasn't necessary, maybe not even reasonable, in this particular situation. But there's a bigger picture to look at here. Because when a young man learns to stick to what he says—no matter the personal cost—he's well on his way to establishing his reputation as someone people can count on. Someone people can trust.

So encourage your son to be the kind of guy who keeps his word, and commend him when he does!

I like your competitive, *fighting* spirit.

Competition is good. Full stop! We live in a culture that often frowns on the competitive spirit, yet the world is one competitive place. To diminish this most ubiquitous reality of life is to handicap a child by making him misunderstand the culture he will inevitably encounter.

As a matter of practical reality, evil exists in this world, competing for dominance with all that is good. Competing is not optional!

When properly encouraged with biblical values, competition is also profoundly positive and formative. Life is an endless string of wins and losses. Your son needs to learn to be a humble winner and to be gracious if he loses. He was made to compete, even if only against himself. When you see the fighting spirit in his eye, encourage it.

I love listening to you. What you have to say is *always* interesting to me.

From where I was standing, I could see our oldest son—then in his early teen years—sitting alone on the front porch. I had so much on my plate that day that I nearly kept going on to my destination: the laundry room. But something made me stop.

I stepped out the front door, quietly tucking myself between him and the fragrant honeysuckle, and asked him what was on his mind. He started out slow. He mentioned this and that, but then he really got going, and his thoughts poured out for over a half hour. They kept pouring and pouring until he suddenly became self-conscious and started apologizing for his rambling.

But I knew better by then.

When he was younger, I probably would've considered his chattiness more of an interruption to my day than anything. But the more experience I have as a parent, the more I realize that listening says love and that often quality conversation grows out of quantity conversation. Our son needed to know that I found him, and his thoughts, very interesting.

Don't underestimate the power of listening to your son. Make sure you communicate to him that you're not only willing to listen but you're also thrilled to hear whatever thoughts or feelings he wants to share with you.

I've got to hand it to you— you've sure got guts.

Persevering against difficult odds takes grit. Continuing on when others have given up because of fear or they've stopped believing it could be done takes determination. It takes guts. Your son coping well with a demanding, difficult situation shows his inner strength.

He needs to know that you see the strength of his character— that he was willing to take on a big challenge and didn't shrink back. In becoming a man, your son wants to feel your respect, and he needs to hear that you respect him too. It's not enough that you're bursting with pride and feel immense admiration on the inside. You must speak your heart into his.

Wow, son, you're so *smart*.

I can't tell you how many men I've met who, at some point, have confided that they didn't consider themselves very smart. And I'm always quite surprised to hear it, because inevitably it's some guy I admire for the way his mind works.

So what happened? What gave them the idea, even into adulthood, that they didn't have enough going on upstairs when in truth they clearly have very sharp minds? If our conversation continued, it usually came out that they didn't get high grades in school or that what they did achieve was never good enough for their parents (or other influential people in their lives).

Such a tragedy.

Because it is evident to everyone else around them that they are plenty smart—maybe not particularly in regard to academics, but they're definitely intelligent.

Don't assume your son realizes how smart he really is. Point out to him all the different ways he is using his brain, not only when it comes to schoolwork but also in many other ways. Is he a good problem solver? Is he creative with his words or his hands?

Build up your son by telling him all the wonderful ways he uses his mind!

You are a young man
with *self-discipline!*

Self-discipline in boys/young men is highly commendable, as it is rare. Whether it's regarding a chore, a sport, a project, or working out—whatever it is—when you observe your son displaying self-discipline, let him know you see his choices and priorities and are very proud.

The man who won't govern himself is in training to be governed by others. The man who rules himself is a man preparing for success in life.

You have a *winning* smile.

A friend of ours who's a builder asked one of our sons to help out at a job site. We wondered how he'd do, never having done that kind of work before. He came home tired, dirty, and with a few aching muscles, but he said he'd felt good about the day.

The next day he got up while it was still dark and went out to do it again.

After a few weeks of this, we got a message from his boss and our friend. He told us that he liked working with "this kid," not only because he was a hard worker but also because he had such a great smile when asked to do any task.

My husband and I had to laugh. I can't tell you how much we'd emphasized the importance of a smile in this boy's life. Because for some reason, it just didn't seem to come naturally to him. We'd even show him pictures of when we "caught" him smiling so he could see for himself what a difference it made. His whole face lights up when he smiles!

Now here it was coming from someone other than his parents, and it turned out that his smile had a big impact on how he was perceived at work, literally affecting his standing at a job that was important to him.

We want our sons to realize the power of a happy countenance. And a great place to start is by complimenting him on his winning smile!

You have *vision*: the ability to see past what is to what is possible.

Everyone needs vision to thrive, but not everyone has a vision. To have vision is to see a mark on the horizon—a goal, a destiny, a purpose, and a priority. In Proverbs 29:18, the Bible says, "Where there is no vision, the people perish" (KJV).

For a meaningful, fulfilled life, the ability to see past today is necessary. Vision is about possibilities, and this takes some time and experience to develop. Embrace the process and allow your son to travel the path of his journey. At some point his vision will come into razor-sharp focus. Until then, encourage him by being open and positive about his thoughts and ideas.

You are such a *tender* warrior.

Maybe your boy is different from ours, but all four of our sons—
even with the contrasts between their personalities—enjoy
watching warriors giving it all they've got on the movie screen,
whether it's ninjas, Avengers, or Stormtroopers. And we certainly understand the draw.

As parents of growing young men, we recognize that each of
them has a warrior deep down inside and embrace their desire
to fight hard for all that's right and good. But we want to help our
sons value their compassionate side as well.

We've watched our boys' eyes fill with tears when they've
witnessed an injustice or a wounding, and we've encouraged
them to understand that their emotions are understandable
and appropriate. A young man can be both tenderhearted and a
fighter—there's no need to pick one or the other.

Talk to your son about both "sides" of his heart—the side
that's ready to do battle and the tender side that brings tears to
his eyes. Tell him how much you admire your tender warrior.

You don't let obstacles stop you, and that's why you're going to go far.

A child needs to know he's going to make it, that he's going to succeed. And it's immensely powerful when his parents believe it first!

In a moment of problem-solving, show your son that he can have the mindset to overcome an obstacle. Remind him that men who accomplish their goals are not defeated by obstacles; they are determined to conquer those obstacles to achieve their goals.

We have two sayings in our home that go way back: "Jacobsons never give up" and "There's always a way to get something done." True, these approaches must be tempered by God's direction/redirection through the leading of the Holy Spirit, but from an early age, we sought to instill a can-do spirit in our children, encouraging them to persevere and not to give up.

This way of thinking will stand them in good stead in any sphere of life—sports, business, and the walk of faith.

I love your *creativity* and how you think outside the box.

At first the answer seemed obvious, at least it did to me. I grew impatient as I watched our second-to-last son go to great lengths to create a rather complex solution to a basic problem. He started out by trying his old school glue, then rummaged around until he found a sturdy rubber band. Then, before I knew it, he'd run out to the toolshed and returned carrying Gorilla Glue, duct tape, and some other gadget I couldn't even identify.

I rolled my eyes and called out to him, "What are you doing with all of that, son?" Honestly! He only grinned back, seemingly oblivious to my exasperation. "I'm gonna fix it, Mom!"

My suggestion was that he solve everything by throwing the whole thing into the trash. But he wasn't about to give up, not a chance. He fiddled and fiddled, never appearing discouraged by his lack of progress.

The way I generally think is if a thing doesn't work, it doesn't work. But that's not how he sees it. For him, an aggravating problem is merely an opportunity for the creative juices to start flowing.

And I love that about him. He's always ready to think outside the box, and our world needs more of these kinds of thinkers (even if they do end up bringing the entire contents of the tool-shed into the house).

So if you have the kind of kid who thinks of solutions or sees angles that others don't see, be sure to encourage him to keep up the excellent work. We could all use some creative thinkers like him.

Apologizing and asking forgiveness take *real* humility. You chose God's way, and it was awesome to see.

Most people find apologizing and asking forgiveness to be excruciatingly painful, which is easy to understand. It's hard to say no to our pride. Our flesh would rather choose anything else before choosing to be humble. But this is God's requirement—that we be humble. According to Proverbs 22:4,

> By humility and the fear of the Lord
> Are riches and honor and life. (NKJV)

So, in that moment, when your son genuinely humbles himself and asks for forgiveness, help him see he chose God's way—the way of real success, from God's perspective.

You're a *good sport.*

You wouldn't think middle school basketball could be such a big deal, especially at a private Christian school in a relatively small town like ours. But then again, you might be surprised. Those country basketball competitions can get fairly intense!

And I may or may not have been one of those mothers on the sidelines yelling and cheering my head off—a side of me I'm not sure I even knew existed before basketball season hit. But when the score was tied and only a few minutes were left in the game, I could hardly breathe and barely stand to watch.

Yet, eventually, one team won and the other did not.

I could see our youngest son out on the court, and I knew how badly he'd wanted to win this game in particular. And I wondered how he'd respond. No one else noticed the emotion in his eyes as fans from the other team exploded with great excitement while those from his losing team displayed deep disappointment. But I saw it. Then I watched him quickly swipe his hand across his cheek and get in line to congratulate the winning team.

We later talked about the game when we were alone in the car on the way home. His father and I commended him for keeping his cool even though it was a tough loss. He confessed that's not how he was feeling on the inside at the time, but he knew it was the right thing to do.

There will be many situations in life when we don't win and won't be number one. Yet the Bible instructs us to "rejoice with those who rejoice" (Rom. 12:15), which is sometimes easier said than done. So be sure to call it out when you see your son handling his losses well. Cheer for him when he's the winner. Cheer even louder, however, when he's not but is still determined to be a good sport about it!

You're learning to save your money, making you a *wise* man who will have options in the future.

As every parent knows, there will always be a thousand reasons to spend all your money. Teaching kids to save is a challenge. And, at some point, your son will have to make his own decisions and heed or ignore your advice. But you can encourage him from a young age. Has he saved some money? He is to be commended! No matter how small the amount, the fact that he put some aside shows discipline and prudence.

Praise him and help him see the connection between saving and options in the future.

You have a passion for justice, and this world is in *desperate* need of people like you.

Our oldest son was born with a strong sense of justice, and you could see it in him from an early age. He's always looking out for anyone who might be weaker or who struggles. He'll protect them or come alongside them so they aren't alone.

This son clearly has a gentle, tender side. But he also has a warrior side that makes him willing to fight for what's right and to see that justice is carried out (if he has anything to say about it). When he was a young boy, it was sweet to watch, but now that he's grown up, it's more than sweet; it's powerful.

In addition to holding a full-time job, he recently started his own candle company along with a friend where part of the proceeds goes to help fight human trafficking. These young men wanted something to match their vision of peace, warmth, and protection, and these candles have brought that to life.

Micah 6:8 instructs us,

> He has told you, O man, what is good;
>   and what does the LORD require of you
> but to do justice, and to love kindness,
>   and to walk humbly with your God?

What could be more encouraging than to see a younger generation do what they can to make a real difference in this world?

I love that you're *ambitious* and can't wait to see where it will take you.

Kids with ambition and a strong drive can be exhausting! When our sons are young, they often have enthusiasm for things other than what we want them to be passionate about. Let's start by reminding ourselves that drive and ambition are good things—aspects of a mindset to be encouraged, not diminished.

Remember that journey your son is on? There are many side roads, but for the most part, with gentle guidance from you, those side roads lead right back to that forward trajectory of maturity and God's perfect plan. As parents, let's strongly encourage drive while taking care not to crush ambition. Gently direct them toward the right path and good purposes.

You're learning to manage your time, and that's a mark of *maturity.*

Our son had so many fun plans scheduled for the weekend that I wondered how he could possibly get his term paper written by Monday morning. Like every good mother, I couldn't help but give him a little nudge.

"Son," I said, "are you sure your paper will be ready to turn in on time?"

"Oh, yes," he assured me. Apparently he had everything well in hand. And all seemed fine, right up until Sunday night. Then reality set in.

Although he had started the paper the week before, he'd assumed the rest would simply "flow" once he put his mind to it. But it didn't exactly go like that. So there he was at 10:00 p.m. on Sunday, with only 250 of the assigned 750 to 1,000 words written. I tiptoed into his room to check his progress and saw the panic—and the accompanying emotion—in his eyes. He was paying the price for his procrastination, and there wasn't anything anyone could do about it now.

My mother's heart ached for him. How I'd wanted to prevent this moment all weekend long. Everything in me had said to help him out and make him sit down to work on the paper. But his father had wisely stopped me, knowing our son was old enough to figure these things out for himself, and I'd simply had to resist the impulse to rescue him.

In the end, our son turned in a completed paper. But he had to stay up much of the night to finish it, and we all knew it was hardly his best work and would affect his grade accordingly. A lesson learned. It may not have been the last lesson either, but it was still a good one for a young man.

I know I'm not the only mother who's wanted to save her son from a bad choice. Many parents tend to manage their children's time for them, but even when they are young, we can start giving them room to govern themselves. If we're willing to do that, then we're preparing them for a great future. Time management is an important skill for our sons to develop, and we can help encourage them when we see them spending time wisely.

Your impulse was to show *mercy,* and I know that pleases God.

Mercy—it's not typically the first word that comes to mind when talking about young boys. And yet how powerfully we speak into our son's life and thoughts when we observe him genuinely showing mercy and offering a kind response to someone in need.

One game our daughter with special needs can play is Uno, and our fourteen-year-old son is often willing to play with her. The truth is, they're both pretty sharp, but, obviously, he has a distinct advantage. But you'd never know it when they play—it's always neck and neck. He makes sure of it. In any other competition, he's a shark and loves to win, but when it comes to playing Uno with her, he has a heart like melted butter. I love his compassion and mercy.

This behavior wasn't automatic. It was something he grew into. That's why we need to find those moments. Was your son merciful, even in the smallest way? Let him know how grateful you are to him for that moment. Let him know that God looks down from heaven, well pleased.

I admire your *eager* mind.

The young boy followed me into the laundry room. He and his family were over at our house for dinner that evening, and I'd slipped in there to put something away when I noticed the little follower behind me. I'd never thought of our laundry room as a particularly exciting place and figured he'd get bored in a minute or two.

But I called that one wrong. This little guy seemed absolutely fascinated by the place. He peppered me with all kinds of questions. "What do you do in here?" and "What's in that drawer?" and "How about that cupboard?" Before I was done answering one question, he was already on to the next one. I told him about the medicines we kept in one spot and a variety of cleaning supplies kept elsewhere: he was intrigued by it all.

At some point, the young boy's mom came looking for him and found us discussing the many mysteries of our resident junk drawer. She seemed a bit embarrassed and immediately started apologizing that her son was pestering me with so many questions. I reassured her that it wasn't a bother in the least. Her son's inquisitiveness was merely an indication of his obvious intelligence, and it was a joy to answer him.

She paused for a moment to consider my unexpected response. Like so many tired moms of little boys, she had not realized, or maybe had temporarily forgotten, that her son's curiosity was a gift, not a nonstop source of exhaustion (although it can sometimes feel that way when you're the parent). Then I could see this sweet mom taking note, and my guess is that she would look at his never-ending questions with renewed patience going forward.

So as a parent of the highly inquisitive, try to remember you'll want to encourage your son's curiosity. We never want our sons to perceive themselves as a bother or pain. Rather than being annoyed by the nonstop questions, tell him it's something you admire about him!

You have a *positive* influence on others, and that's powerful.

I watched the two young boys as they started stirring up trouble at school. My chair was in the back of the classroom, so I guess they didn't realize I could see them from where I sat. Or maybe they just didn't care. Usually their antics were relatively harmless, but this one day they got a little carried away, and I was genuinely concerned.

I wondered if I should say anything, and what I should say if I did.

As I spent a minute deliberating what to do, I observed their other classmate, who happened to be one of our sons, call them out. But he spoke to them offhandedly, even with a slight laugh. "Hey, guys, you don't really want to do that, do you?"

His point was both well-made and surprisingly well-taken.

I suppose it's hard for a twelve-year-old boy to believe he has any kind of influence whatsoever, but he does. So does your nine-year-old, and even a four-year-old can positively impact his young friends and companions.

Your son might not realize he's having an influence on those around him, but you can help him see that he is and that it's making a difference in the world—at the very least in the world around him.

Your *enthusiasm* and *energy* bring life to the room.

Our oldest son was born with seemingly limitless energy. He always woke up early and bright-eyed, ready to take on the world . . . and stayed that way until he finally crashed into bed at night.

And to be perfectly honest, it was exhausting.

But I clearly remember once when a friend overheard me moaning on a day when it felt like it was almost too much to take. "Why can't he just quietly color at the table like other children?" I asked. And she admonished me on the spot. She'd observed these kinds of kids over the years and could see what I could not.

"Why are you complaining about this child who's so full of strength and life? Isn't that what you're going to want around you in your old age? Isn't that what you're going to want out there in the world someday?"

She gave me a lot to think about that day. And now that our son is an adult, he's not only a comfort "in my old age" but also so much more. He is incredibly helpful and supportive, and we're thankful for his seemingly unwavering energy. He's come through for us in more ways than I can say.

Yes, God knew we'd need the determination and passion of this son someday. And if you too have an energetic son, let me encourage you that it's truly a gift you have there! Make sure he knows how much you love the way he brings life into any room he enters.

I appreciate how you are *learning* to work things out with others.

I was deeply immersed in reading a good book out on the back patio when I heard the door slam. Startled, I looked up to see one of our younger sons striding angrily out the back door. Before I had a chance to ask, the door flew open again and his older brother called out to him, "Hey, we're not done with the conversation!" But his younger brother ignored him and kept walking.

Although I typically give the boys a chance to work out their differences, I interceded on this one. I stopped our younger son and quietly—but firmly—told him this was *not* how we do things in our family. We do not walk away from the other person. We stay and try to work it out.

Oh, maybe it didn't seem like all that big of a deal because it was just his brother, but then again, here was a great chance for him to practice with his family how to show love and respect to others—no matter how he's feeling.

Since that day, I've observed several times when this same son started to walk away from a difficult conversation and then suddenly stopped and turned back around. He still has growing to do in this area, but he's slowly learning to stay in the game and work things through with others.

When you see your son trying hard to communicate and work things out with others, be sure to acknowledge him. It will give him the confidence he needs to continue engaging with others in that way.

I like how *careful* you are in choosing your friends.

From an early age we noticed our youngest son was slow in making friends. Because he's naturally an outgoing and good-natured guy, we also found it slightly surprising. Why wasn't he quickly making friends with the other boys in his class? Why didn't he readily join that group of guys who hung out together during lunch and breaks?

Our son wasn't a shy kid, so it didn't make any sense to his dad or me.

I finally asked him about it, not wanting to make him feel self-conscious but also wanting to understand what was going on in his head.

His answer went something like this: "Mom, I like most all the kids in my class, so I'm pretty much friends with everyone." He paused, then continued, saying, "But when it comes to true friends, close friends, I want to make sure he's got qualities that I admire and can trust. So I've been holding back a bit to see who that might be."

And I felt slightly convicted. Here I was so concerned about him fitting in and making a lot of friends, while he was appraising character when it came to cultivating a close friendship.

While it's lovely to be friendly to the many people around you, it's also wise to be careful about who you choose to go deep with and trust in. Encourage your son in both.

You're a *real* team player.

Knowing how to get along with others to accomplish a common goal is essential to success in life. That's why Lisa and I seek opportunities for our boys to work together. Without cooperation, everything takes three times as long. I give them a job and step back, allowing them to figure out how to tackle it.

Today, it was window washing. We live in a two-story house with lots of windows. "Boys," I said, "the windows need to be washed. Let me know if you need any input." And I left it at that. It ended better than it started, but they got the job done in a few hours and were proud of what they'd accomplished together. If your boys are young, you can achieve the same goals with different, more age-appropriate circumstances.

We must teach our sons the importance of working together, and there's nothing like real-life circumstances to put that teaching to the test. When your son shows a cooperative spirit, let him know you noticed. Let him know you are proud of him.

Your generosity is a *loving gift* to many.

Maybe it's because there are ten people in our family, but we tend to keep our birthday celebrations simple and relatively small. We don't throw expensive parties or give lavish gifts (remember, everything is times ten!). Of course, we try to be thoughtful, but our presents often include basics such as a specialty T-shirt, a fun game, or a coffee shop gift card.

You can imagine my surprise when I saw a rather large gift box sitting in front of me on my birthday. I was even more astonished when I learned it was from our thirteen-year-old son. What could it be? I slowly pulled back the wrapping paper and opened the box to find a beautiful wooden diffuser. I knew it must have cost him at least forty dollars—a rather significant portion of his budget.

And it was all I could do not to protest! He really shouldn't have splurged on me.

But I stopped when I saw his face expectantly watching for my response to his gift of love. This was not the moment to lecture him about wise budgeting, because this was about expressing extravagant love. Here was a young man determined to bless his mom with a special birthday gift. And sometimes generosity can be the greatest gift.

If you have a son who tends to be generous, I hope you'll let him know what a blessing he is to you and everyone around him.

You are a *strong* role model for those around you.

When your son does something—it can be anything—that is right and good, it's the perfect opportunity to help him see the much larger role he will play in the world someday. Thoughts lead to decisions, and decisions lead to actions—it's all connected. And it's not merely an internal matter affecting only him. He is connected with his brothers and sisters and friends—even people who see him act correctly or righteously (or wrongly!) in the park, people who may never know him personally.

The world may be "going by," but it's also observing us as it does. How we live and act is seen by others. Helping your son realize the big picture will elevate his consciousness of how he impacts others by how he lives. And it's always best to help him make this connection on the positive side of his behavior. Tell him he is providing an excellent example of how a young man should live. Tell him he is a strong role model.

I appreciate the way you're *careful* not to talk negatively about other people.

I walked into the classroom only a few minutes after the event occurred, but it was clear that something had gone on before I'd come in. Some of the students were giggling, but most were looking away and pretending like nothing had happened. But it was quite apparent by the look on the teacher's face that something had gone on—and it wasn't good.

As there were only a few minutes left of the school day, I waited until we were in the car and heading home before I asked our son about it. "Hey, do you want to tell me what went on in the classroom before I arrived?"

Our son looked uncomfortable, then shrugged.

So I tried asking about it in another way. I even went so far as to throw out a few students' names that I thought might have been involved. But he still seemed hesitant to say anything. Then he explained to me, "It's not that I wouldn't tell you everything, Mom, but I don't want to talk badly about the other kids. They're usually pretty good kids, but it's true they got carried away with something silly today."

Then he added, "And that happens to me sometimes too."

I thought about what he'd said. And, frankly, I was convicted and wondered if I always gave as much grace to others as I'd want to be given to me.

Tell your son that you appreciate how he avoids talking badly about others and what a terrific quality it is to have in a young man.

You have such a *positive*, helpful attitude, and it's *super* encouraging to me.

Of course, his attitude isn't always positive, is it? Often his attitude in response to your request needs to be corrected. But there are also moments when your son will respond correctly, and when he does, make sure you point it out and express your gratefulness for it. Positive reinforcement of praiseworthy moments builds up your relationship and focuses your son's thoughts on the praise you have communicated.

Certainly, you could quote Bible verses to him when he chooses to respond negatively, but we all know how that will turn out, don't we? If you do have to correct him and teach him how he was wrong in the moment, be sure to do it during a neutral time—not in the moment of emotional intensity. But by finding the moments to praise him and focusing on those, you'll discover that the need for correction will diminish greatly and your relationship will deepen.

I'm *grateful* for your servant's heart.

We woke up one morning to an unexpectedly heavy snow, and on top of that, most of us were struggling with severe colds. So as much as our family hates to miss church, it was clear that we couldn't attend on this particular Sunday.

But when our daughter with special needs heard the news, she quickly broke down in tears. Going to church is the highlight of her week and although, thankfully, she hadn't come down with the cold, the rest of us were in pretty bad shape with sniffles and sneezes. We tried to explain to our dear girl why this meant she couldn't go either, but it sure didn't make any sense in her mind.

Then, just as she was nearing despair, her younger teenage brother spoke up. He said, "Don't worry, I'll take her. I'm not feeling too bad, and I don't want her to miss out if she doesn't have to."

While we were grateful for his kind offer, we hesitated. It's no small task to wheel her through the snow and then heave her little, helpless body into the truck.

"Are you sure?" we asked. "You don't really have to, you know."

But he seemed quite determined, and so we watched from the front porch as he steered her wheelchair down the snowy ramp and hoisted her into the old four-wheel-drive truck. Off they went, with her smiling and waving wildly through the ice-covered window. It was enough to warm any heart, no matter what the temperature was outside.

So if you have a son with a strong servant's heart, be sure to thank him. He has no idea how many people he will bless or hearts he will warm in the years to come.

No matter how challenging life is or what goes wrong, the sun will rise tomorrow, and there is *always hope.*

Loss—it's a part of life. As loving parents, we always desire to shield our children from the worst of what life dishes out, don't we? But when our fifth baby had a massive stroke just prior to birth, there was no way to shield our other four young children from what had happened. We kept telling our kids, all under the age of seven, that our little baby was "special." Then one day the reality dawned on our daughter, and she burst out through angry, painful tears, "Well, that doesn't sound very special!" She was right too; it doesn't sound that way.

Our baby's birth story was devastating to us and so hard to explain in any way that made sense to our young children. All we could do was point to hope. Faith was all we had. God always has a plan and a purpose, even if we can't see that purpose in the moment.

Put your arm around your son and remind him that the sun will rise tomorrow. God is still in control. He has a plan and wants us to put our trust in Him.

You are so brave, and I'm *proud* of you.

We live in the country and keep laying hens (and a lot of other animals over the years), which always interest coyotes. If you've never heard the yipping, yowling, barking cries of coyotes at night, it can be unnerving, especially for young children. The reality is that coyotes are totally fearful of people and don't pose a threat. But that fact doesn't matter when you're nine, it's winter, night comes early, and you forgot to fill up the woodbox earlier in the day.

As the coyotes struck up a chorus so loud that they may as well have been in our front room, our son stood at the door staring at the handle.

"Would you like me to go with you, son?" I asked.

He hesitated for a moment as I shifted in my chair, getting up to join him.

"No, Dad, I'm okay," he said as he opened the door and stepped into the night.

With his first step crunching on the snow, the coyotes immediately stopped and all was still. Moments later, he walked in, arms full of chopped wood and a look of settled confidence on his face.

"Son, you are so brave!"

Every family's life is different, but every life has moments when bravery is called for. You might not live in the country, but does Mom need a spider removed from the bathroom? Look for any chance to compliment your son's bravery, no matter how small or seemingly insignificant the circumstance. He who is recognized as brave will continue to cultivate bravery throughout his life. And that's what you want for your son, isn't it?

You will never be alone. I will *always* be here for you, and God will never abandon you.

Sometimes there's a conflict in what our son feels and what is true. And there comes a time more than once in a young man's life when he feels alone on the journey. *Nobody cares, nobody understands*, the voices in his head repeatedly tell him. It's a silent kind of pain, of suffering, but that doesn't diminish the brutal stabbing at his heart.

Listen. Even if he isn't saying anything. Simply be with him and listen to the silence together. Be patient. At some point, the dam will break, and he will open his heart to you.

When you discern the moment is right, help him understand that you will always be at his side, defending, supporting, and warring with him. And then remind him of an important truth: Jesus knows exactly what it feels like to be abandoned, to feel all alone. He had been traveling with and teaching His disciples for over three years. Then they made the journey from the garden of Gethsemane to the cross, and on the journey, every disciple, after pronouncements of faithfulness and support, abandoned Him. Even Peter, the most vocal of them all, started cursing and saying he wasn't with Jesus—didn't even know Him. How that must have cut Jesus to the bone. Jesus knows what it is like to be alone.

Hebrews 4:15 says, "For we have not an high priest which

cannot be touched with the feeling of our infirmities; but was in all points tempted like as we are, yet without sin" (KJV).

Jesus understands the things we face in this life. And we have an amazing promise from God: "I will never leave you nor forsake you" (Heb. 13:5).

Even in the valley, in the darkest, most alone-feeling time, God promises that He is there with you. And that is an encouraging truth.

Matt Jacobson was an executive in the publishing industry for twenty-five years and for the past seventeen years has been a teaching elder/pastor at Cline Falls Bible Fellowship. Matt is the founder of FaithfulMan.com, an online social media community focusing on the topics of marriage, parenting, and biblical teaching. He is the cohost of the *FAITHFUL LIFE* podcast with his wife, Lisa, and the author of *100 Words of Affirmation Your Wife Needs to Hear*.

Matt also created the Freedom Course (Freedom.Faithfulman .com), a program that teaches men to be true to the faith and faithful to their wives, and how to find real freedom from and real victory over sexual sin and pornography.

Lisa Jacobson is an author, a speaker, and the founder and host of Club31Women.com, an online community of Christian women authors who write weekly on the topics of marriage, home, family, and biblical truths—a powerful voice for biblical womanhood. She is the cohost of the *FAITHFUL LIFE* podcast with her husband, Matt, and the author of *100 Words of Affirmation Your Husband Needs to Hear*. Matt and Lisa live in the Pacific Northwest, where they have raised their eight children.

Connect with
Lisa and *Club31Women!*

Club31Women.com

Cohost of the *FAITHFUL LIFE* Podcast

@Club31Women

Connect with
MATT and FAITHFUL MAN!

FaithfulMan.com
BiblicalMarriageCoach.com

Cohost of the *FAITHFUL LIFE* Podcast

@FaithfulMan

Hands-on advice
to *LOVE* one another better.

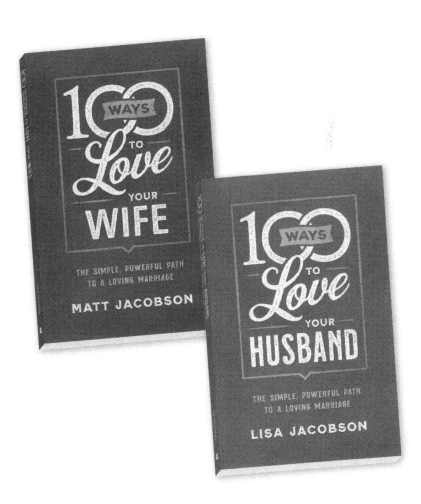

Encouragement to tell your spouse *TODAY*.

Powerful Ways to
BUILD UP YOUR DAUGHTER

One hundred phrases to say to your daughter that
deeply encourage, affirm, and inspire. Start speaking
these words into her life and watch your child—and your
relationship with her—transform before your eyes.

R Revell
a division of Baker Publishing Group
www.RevellBooks.com

Available wherever books and ebooks are sold.

Printed in Great Britain
by Amazon

16966724R00075